Table of Contents

Chapter 1 – What is Branding?

Chapter 2 – Branding Basics

Chapter 3 – Audience

Chapter 4 – Logos

Chapter 5 – Building Recognition

Chapter 6 – Competition

Chapter 7 – Establishing Brand

Chapter 8 – Establishing Company Identity

Chapter 9 – Media Consideration

Chapter 10 – The Competitive Edge

Chapter 12 – Reinforcement of Your Brand

Chapter 1 – What is Branding?

Branding is all about image of a business. The concept doesn't only include style, emblems and logos but also the image of quality perceived. The image perceived may be of total quality, reliability, and more.

Branding is about the business and how a business is different from the competitors. The purpose of a brand is to distinguish yourself from your competitors. Once you make a distinguishing impact then an advertising campaign can be much more effective.

The success of a company can be determined by a brand. Branding includes many factors, which help a company be successful. These factors may include a website, marketing efforts, and anything that gives a company an identity. Consumers trust wholeheartedly a corporate image because there is a psychology in motivating the purchasing decisions.

All companies should practice branding. Brick and mortar business and online companies benefit through branding methods. It is common for smaller companies and online businesses to fail due to a lack of understanding about the importance and factors of a good brand.

Branding ensures professionalism with a company. It seals the deal on an entire package. A small company with a brand looks just as good as a large corporation when they practice the right techniques. Brands enhance your confidence as a business owner but also in the consumers that you really can deliver what you promise.

Branding offers consistency with a business. It gives direction to employees and customers know what to expect.

Consistency can be performed through the use of things like business cards, t-shirts, and more. Consistency includes visibility techniques that are professional and will remain in the memory of a consumer.

One concept that consumers often attach to a brand is called brand equity. A brand is often considered to be an asset also. For example, if you have developed a very good brand that is well known as being a top distributor of massage chairs and you have a competitor with a brand known to provide defective products, your brand will be worth more.

Chapter 2 – Branding Basics

Branding is all about what the customers perceive of your company. Your brand is the promise that you intend to make to the customers. The ultimate goal is to spark an emotional connection in order to create a positive feeling resulting of loyalty to a specific product from the customers.

Most customers hold true to products they enjoy. It is very common for a customer to be impressed with a brand and continue to buy a product based on that brand. You want to create these feelings of loyalty to bring the customers back for more. This is the ultimate goal.

Mission and Vision of Your Company

The mission and vision of your company should uphold excellence in providing a quality product to customers that you care about. These are statements about your company regarding the ultimate goals you wish to achieve with in your endeavors. Many companies focus their vision or mission on their employees while others extend their mission outward to the customers. There should be a fine mix here with both.

Many customers do not read into a vision or mission statement too often. However, that doesn't mean that you shouldn't take it seriously. Your vision and mission are both a part of the branding process because they define what your company is all about. These two statements need to be believed and practiced by employees and all staff of the company.

Benefits and Features of Your Products or Services

A big part of creating a brand for your business is proving to the customers why your products and services are the best to buy. Differentiation takes place here but you need to prove the benefits to the consumers. Determine what the benefits are with the products you offer, the services you offer, or something else. Why does the customer benefit when they shop or buy from you? You will have a very hard time establishing a brand if you cannot determine the benefits or your products or services.

The features of your products and services are also important and they go hand in hand with the benefits. The features of a specific product should provide a benefit. Determine the features and the ones that stand out from the rest or provide the biggest benefit may be a target for the marketing campaign.

Customers Perception Today

Branding is about customer's perception. When you want to create a brand you want to create a perception of the customer that you are the best, provide quality, or maybe even more.

It is important to have a good idea of what the customers currently think of you when you are building a branding campaign. Today customers may not know that you exist or they may have a negative feel for your business because you haven't been practicing proper methods. Have a clear understanding on exactly what the customers think of you.

If you are unsure what the customers think of you then you may need to send out surveys and questionnaires. These types of things can help you get a good idea where you stand with the perception of the customers. It is okay if it is bad today. It will give you something to build on with your branding campaign.

Qualities Perceived by the Customers

The next thing you need to do with a branding campaign is to determine the different qualities that are perceived about your products by the customers. Do you have a good reputation with the consumer world for providing total quality in your products or are your products considered to be garbage and not worth the money?

The qualities of your business may be many things. When you think about how customers consider the qualities of your business, make sure you consider the products you offer, the customer support you provide, your image, or anything else that would make a customer think of quality coming from your company.

The vision and mission statement are very important for every business no matter how big or small. Make sure that your brand works well and matches what you say you want to deliver. Determine what the benefits and features of your business are and have a clear picture on this. You will need this information to provide a clear picture when you focus on developing your brand.

Also learn about what the customers really think of you. You might think customers absolutely love you when they are really bashing you on the quality of your product. Knowing what the customers think is very important. Creating a brand based on customer input can be successful, especially if you change the design of something for the customers. This gives them a sense of ownership and it shows them you really do care.

Chapter 3 – Audience

Audience is everything. If you do not know the audience that you are targeting then you cannot begin creating a brand for a product or a company. There are many reasons that audience must be considered. Knowing your audience well will work for you in the long run.

The audience is the targeted customer base that you are hoping to reach out to for purchasing your product. Audience may include gender, age, geographical regions, and more.

The age of an audience must be considered when branding occurs. This is because if you are targeting a younger and more hip crowd they may want to see a brand that is vibrant and more hip. If your audience is older and more sophisticated then they may be looking for a brand displaying more professionalism.

Gender of an audience is often an issue if you are selling women's clothing, men's hats, or other items. However, when you create a brand for a man, remember that you can create ad campaigns targeting the women to purchase the products as gifts for men.

Income isn't something that many people think about when they consider an audience when developing a brand. This is often where companies go wrong. If you are selling a video gaming system that is several hundreds of dollars in a local store down the street and the average income of families in the area is less than $25,000 a year they may not be able to afford the product. You cannot sell an expensive product to a poor audience. Also, people with a very high income may not consider purchasing a very cheap product. The value of your brand must match the income of the people you think will be your primary target as customers.

Geographical regions are also very important. Many people open businesses and try to sell products and services where there just isn't a need. This is a good way to fail. For example, if you have a company selling snow shovels then it wouldn't make sense to try to sell them to homeowners in Florida. Know your geographical locations and which regions will benefit the most from your product or services.

Know Your Audience

There are many things about your audience that you must know when you are creating a brand. If you do not have a clear understanding of which your audience is then you will fail.

When you determine your audience it is important to narrow it down based on the age, gender (only if specific), geographical region (only if specific), income levels, and more. Your audience will be defined as something like 20-30 year old, male golfers that are left handed.

Some brands may not be this specific. However, the more you can narrow down your audience the more your brand will separate you from the competition. This means you will have less competition to worry about also.

Branding by Your Audience

Branding by your audience will allow you to be more successful with sales and develop long lasting customers that are dedicated to you. Targeting the wrong audience can cause problems with credibility and trust.

Older groups of people often want to see a brand as one

they can trust. They want credibility and a professional look. If the image appears to be young or unprofessional then you may find that your revenues are lacking.

The same practice rings true with a younger crowd. If you are targeting a young crowd and your brand is too professional and comes across as boring then kids will not be interested in what you have to offer. For example, if your target audience is to sell super fast toy cars to five-year-old boys then you want a very exciting brand that is fun. If your brand is professional and so is your appearance it will be hard to convince a 5 year old that the cars are really fast.

Always brand by audience. Find out what they want to see. You may even want to talk to different age groups and find out what they would like to see. This would be a good place to start.

Chapter 4 – Logos

Today it is common for people to say that a logo is everything when it comes to branding. This couldn't be further from the truth. A logo is important in many ways when branding but it is not where the rubber meets the road with a business and a brand. A logo is one of the smallest pieces of branding.

About Logos

It is common for many companies not to have a logo at all with their company. They may just have the name of their business in bright and basic letters in front of the store. Many online site owners do the same and just write the name of the website in bold letters at the top. A logo is important for every company and a good idea to have.

A logo may be a creative way of writing your company name in bold or italic lettering, special font, different colors, and it may even contain a picture. A good logo is the golden yellow arches in McDonalds. This is a symbol that everyone recognizes when they see the yellow arches on a highway or side street from a distance. People immediately know which restaurant the arches are for.

A logo can be just one letter or it may even be your entire name. Developing a logo may be something you put off until the end of your branding process if you are not sure what you would like it to look like.

Tips with Logos

When you do design a logo there are many things to consider so you know that you are creating a good one. These things include the colors, how busy the logo is, a tagline, memorable, and more.

Colors are very important in a logo. They can be extremely annoying if they are too bright and hard to look at and they can be too dull and boring. It is very important to choose a wise color combination with your logo. Again, consider the audience when you design the logo and choose the colors. A more professional look for an older audience should use lighter tones and pleasing colors while children enjoy primary and bright colors.

A logo should never be too busy. It should be short and sweet. You want a company logo to be simple and easy to remember. A logo that is too busy may be annoying and hard to read.

It is important to search competitor sites and verify that there are no other companies with the same name as yours with a logo that is similar. Make sure that you never copy a logo or use a logo that is almost the same as another company also. This could cause you to be in the middle of a lawsuit if you accidentally design the same thing as someone else.

Does a Logo Really Help You Sell?

There is a lot of hype about logo creation and the web is saturated with companies offering to design the perfect company logo. Logos do not help you sell products. They are not responsible for increasing revenues. No one buys a product because the logo is cool or professionally designed.

Logos do create a positive impact for a business. A company with a logo versus a company that does not have a logo looks more professional and comes across as a more credible place to shop from. This is because a professional logo creates an image. For example, employees wearing plain blue shirts in a store do not look as professional as employees with the same plain blue shirt on and a company logo stamped on the top left chest area of the shirt.

Logos are a part of image. Your goal in branding is to create an image that has an emotional impact when the customers. This doesn't mean to add an emotional picture or throw in a tagline to make people cry. Taglines should have an impact but make a promise you are going to deliver. Pictures should not be in logos at all but if you choose to put one in a logo then make sure that it is very small and not too busy.

Chapter 5 – Building Recognition

Building recognition can be a difficult task in the branding process. There are many ways that you build recognition. However, you must start from within the organization and work your way out to the customers and the competitors.

Corporate Overview

All companies need to write a brief paragraph about the company. Give an overview of the business, how you got started, and what makes you thrive today. The overview should be positive and encouraging. It should also make consumers think you are an excellent place to buy from.

Maybe you donate half of your proceed to a non-profit organization helping cancer. If so, then you would want to let people know here. A corporate overview is read often by most people when it is available. An overview should be included on websites, brochures, press releases, and more.

What is Your Personality?

Your personality has a lot to do with your brand. You should make sure that your personality doesn't overpower your brand too much with the company. For example, if an advertisement or company logo would look excellent in the color yellow but you hate the color yellow then maybe you need to do a check on your personality and how it is interfering with the company brand.

It is very wise for many companies to hire a brand manager so there are not problems with personalities conflicting with a brand. The image of the company needs to be based on what looks good for the company, what is attractive to the customers, and what will sell. Your personality should not mix into the brand.

Some people say that you are your brand and your personality should shine with your brand. However, there is a fine line here with this theory. A branding manager is the best option because this person can help with image and they will have a biased point of view and they will act as a cop with the brand not allowing any personalities to interfere.

Consistency

When you are creating a brand then you need to be consistent. Consistency should take place in everything that you do. Remember, brand is your image and if you are not consistent it will not have a good impact on the consumers. The primary question that you should as yourself is if you deliver everything you promise to your customers. The answer here should always be a yes. Delivery should be consistent at all times.

Chapter 6 – Competition

There are many things to consider about your competition when you are designing a branding campaign. Many businesses fail because they do not consider their competition. You need to do proper research about your competitors, learn what makes you different, why the customers should choose you, and much more.

Researching the Competition

You must always research your competition before you begin your brand. Every business must know who their primary competitors are. It is important to know if your company is on top of the list in the industry or exactly where you stand.

When researching competitors it is important to be thorough and learn everything about them that you can. How are you similar? Do they have the same products as you? What types of ad campaigns to they use that are successful? What campaigns to they use that are failing?

What Sets You Apart From the Competitors?

A very important factor when you are researching competitors of your products and services is that it is that you have that is different. If you have to, make a list of everything you have that they do not and vice versa. Determine what it is about your company that works.

Many the competitors left out a vital piece of information that they should be focusing on the product that they are not. This could be a perfect solution to getting a foot in and immediately ahead of the competitors.

When you determine the positive aspect that is different that sets you completely apart from the competitors it may be this information used for your ad campaign.

You never want to look the same as the rest of the companies in your industry. Don't be afraid to step outside of the box and go different. This is how consumers will remember you. If you all look the same then it will be no difference to the customers when they make a choice that they are going to buy from.

Why Should Customers Shop From You?

Another part about setting yourself apart from the competitors is determining why the customers should shop from you and not the other guy. What is it about your business that makes you the right place to shop from?

If you offer sales or free shipping and the competitors don't then you should use this as a focal point right up front. If you have a product that the competitor doesn't then you should use this too. Show the customers why you are the better place. There are many ways to do this. You may have a customer service team that is available 24 hours a day and the other companies may only be open during normal business hours. This would be a focal point.

The reasons that customers should shop from you need to be clear and concise. You need to be entirely different than the rest of the businesses in your industry. Setting yourself apart from the rest is the best thing you can do because it will cause the customers to remember you specifically. There will be no confusion of which company you are in a group of businesses that look the same.

Chapter 7 – Establishing Brand

Once you have determined your mission, vision, audience, and separation from the competitors you can begin to establish your brand. There are many things that you need to do to establish your brand so people will begin to remember your name. These things include getting inside of the customer's mind, get endorsements, find hot prospects, and use the public relations firms to your advantage. These few things will go a long way when making an effort to establish yourself amongst the competition an in the market.

Establishing a Place Inside of the Customer's Mind

One of your biggest goals in the branding process is establishing a place inside of the customer's mind. At this point, you have a good idea who your audience is supposed to be. You know what their income level is, their age, and possibly geographical details. This information is relevant in establishing an actual audience.

Your goal is to prove to the customer they have a need for your product or your service. The customer needs to find a reason why they need you. The branding techniques will tell the customer that your product resolves a problem they may have, fulfills a need they have, and makes their life much better if they purchase it. There has to be a reason to purchase the product and a positive aspect of why it is the best option to use it.

When you get inside of the customer's head the customer will believe they absolutely have to have the product. As you see many infomercials talk about how someone will become rich if they use a product or how their health will be better you need to establish the benefit of the customer so you can make them truly believe that their life will be much better when they use your product.

This also means that you have to build trust and credibility with the customers. Many products do a fantastic job of proving to the customer why a product or service is beneficial and needed. However, they fail to establish credibility or trust with the consumers. Your reputation is not at stake but it is questioned at this point so you need to provide proof that you are going to deliver the promises you are making to the customer.

Endorsements

The public and consumers listen to public figures. When you have the ability to get an endorsement on a product then you need to take advantage of it. However, you cannot wait for an endorsement to come to you. Your public relations manager may need to contact some of these figures to see if they are interested in endorsing a product. One thing to keep in mind is that endorsements may cost quite a bit of money if you are trying to get a public figure to back your product.

There are many ways to get endorsements. You may attend events where a public figure is going to be. This includes getting back stage at concerts or shows where you can have access to the person. You also can call their managers and talk to them about endorsing a product.

One thing to keep in mind about endorsements is that you need to find a figure that matches the audience also. If your target audience is teenagers then you want to find an endorsement that the teenagers know and trust. Someone that the teenagers think is hip and would want to buy the product when they find out the person uses it too. The last thing you would want to do is get an endorsement on your product by an older individual who is well known and respected by an older audience that the teenager audience has never heard of. This would be a waste of money and time on your part.

Hot Prospects

As a marketer, when branding your business or product you need to be on the lookout for hot prospects and opportunities at all times. These need to be taken advantage of when you can. It is important to use every opportunity to get your product exposure in the right methods. These methods may be trade shows or other public events.

When you attend trade shows and other events the goal is to look and be professional. If you just have a table set up with a few products on it then customers may not take you seriously. Attending events like this require professional flyers, banners, signs, and other things to get the attention of attendees. It is important to look prepared and professional.

The more events you attend the more your name gets out there. When you create banners and signs you may find a situation where someone would like to display your banner or sign. Do not charge someone for this. This is a benefit for you because it is free advertising, minus the cost of the banner. It will give you exposure and help you with the branding of your business and product.

Hot prospects need to reach out to the targeted audience for your product or service. Do not attend events that your audience is not going to be at. If there is no way that an elderly crowd will be interested in what you are offering then you are only wasting your time to make a big presentation to them at a trade show. Know who the audience is going to be at the public prospects for gaining exposure.

Using Public Relations Pros to Your Advantage

Media attention needs to be used to your advantage. There are many ways to do this. One thing to keep in mind is that your product and your brand do not have to be fully established yet to gain the attention of the media. What is important is that you use the media to help you get established.

The media can be used in many ways. Press releases are one of the best things you can do to get the exposure you are looking for and help you create a place in the industry of the business.

A press release is usually used for announcing grand openings for new businesses, new product launches, big sales and events, or anything else new that is happening within a company.

The elements of a press release should include the event itself, why people will benefit going to it, the location, date, and time of the event. If you don't tell people where to go it will do you no good. You should also provide your company contact information in case the media wants to call you to get an interview or even write a story on the company. Customers may have questions. Without contact information it could cost you a lot of business. Also, always include your website address in a press release so people can go to your site and learn more about who you are.

Press releases are sent out to as many media outlets as you can send them to for the targeted audiences you are trying to reach out to. These media outlets include news stations, newspapers, magazines, radio stations, and more. When a media outlet receives a press release they may do a few things. They may immediately respond and use it for the next big story that hit the press and tell the public all about it. They may put it aside for when they are waiting for a slow period and then use it as a story or they will do nothing at all.

Sending out press releases doesn't cost a business anything. It is cheap and you do not need to worry about cost. It never hurts to send out press releases even if the media is not interested. The point is that you have to at least try to use public relations to your benefit. It may be that one event or announcement you have about your business that is used by the press. That one small bit of exposure could go a long way for you.

Chapter 8 – Establishing Company Identity

Establishing your identity is very important when you are fighting for a place in a market or a certain niche. You may know exactly who you are but you need to get your name out there and for people to be aware of your existence also. There are many ways you can establish an identity in a local community or around the world.

Donations

Donations do you a lot of justice when it comes to establishing an identity around the local community and anywhere else. Many companies or non-profits offer plaques with your name on them, engravings in the wall, and other things when you donate money to them. This gives you exposure. When customers see your name as a company that made a donation, not only does it look good for you but also it gets the company name out there permanently. This part of the branding process is important because it helps the business build credibility and trust with the customers in the market.

Investments

Investments are very important also. When you invest in a company it is important to be sure they are in the same industry as your product or service. Investing helps build a name for your company, give you more exposure and more. When you invest in a company, one of the agreements you can make when lending your money is that they provide exposure or advertising for you. Investments are very beneficial and help with the branding process.

Give Free Information

So many companies upset customers because they want to charge money for everything. This leaves a customer walking away with a bad taste in their mouth about you and only causes you to look dishonest or greedy. There are things that you can give away for free when it comes to information. There is no way you can teach a customer everything you know in just a few minutes of talking to them or in a few pages that they can read.

Many people practice giving tips and advice through flyers and brochures. You may want to place a few useful tips on the back of your brochure. This will help build credibility and trust with customers that you are not greedy and you are willing to help them achieve certain goals. It will also prove to them that you actually have the knowledge to perform certain tasks within your company. You don't have to reveal secrets of the trade but you can give out helpful information that is useful.

Giving useful information may include offering tips and advice when you are out on a service call in a home. If your company offers plumbing services and you are on a call that the customer has frozen pipes under their home then you may recommend they leave the water dripping overnight. This type of advice is useful to the customer and will help them not end up in a situation with a burst pipe. Although, continuous broken pipes may be a profit for you it is only one customer.

You may think it will not benefit you to tell them how to avoid problems because then they won't need you. However, there are plenty of other reasons they can call you. Plus, you will be the person they will turn to any time they need something repaired. In addition, word of mouth goes a long way with customers and the customer may attract you plenty of business your way.

Adding Value to Your Business

When you are branding it is important to add value with everything you do. Adding value means making yourself valuable to the customers and the community. This may include giving out free information through tips and tricks, statistics, and other useful bits.

You can make the business more valuable by adding a little extra in everything that you do. A voice mail message might include a quick tip on fixing something or a way to prevent a computer virus. The signature on your email should contain more than your name, address, and phone number. You might include a useful sentence underneath that is a quick tip or useful bit of information.

Making yourself useful adds value to your business and to the customers. The customers need to believe that they need you and this is a part of proving to them you are useful and the best person to turn to when they need something.

Getting Your Brand Out There

So you have designed a logo, a name, a tagline, and anything else. Now you need to practice other methods to get your name all over the place. This can be done with clothing, pens, cups, and other paraphernalia.

Clothing is one of the best things you can get out there on people. If you design t-shirts with your company name and logo on them people will wear them. These should be free items that you give away to people as they visit your booth, table, or even take a survey. You may offer the t-shirts to people if they give you feedback on their opinions for certain things. They may provide their information or email, which also is a contact you just made. Always hold onto this information as you can use it in an email campaign. One thing to consider is that when you ask customers for an email address; always ask them if it is okay to contact them via email. Do not assume that it is okay or you may upset them. One thing that is okay is sending a flyer, brochure, or coupon in the regular snail mail.

Clothing works in many ways. People wear free t-shirts all over the world. They may travel to different destinations like a gym working out, a beach, or a fair. This is exposure for you for every person that sees this person. The more t-shirts you get out there the better for your business.

One thing to keep in mind with printed materials as advertising techniques to spread the company name is that you want to create things that are useful for people. A pen with your company name is always useful. Pens will never be thrown away because someone will use them until the ink runs out. They are very cheap to make and easy to distribute. You can give a package of pens to a business that you know spends a lot of time traveling around the world. Before you know it your pens were left in meetings and other places and now you have people checking out your site from other countries. It is as easy as that when you distribute items with your company name on them.

You have to get your name out there and create your popularity. You can do this by designing t-shirts and other useful things for the business. Try to give these things away for free so you can have the best results with your branding.

Also, make sure that the items created look nice and represent your brand, as you want to be portrayed. Match the scheme.

Get One on One with the Customers

Getting one on one with the customers is very important. You need to talk to the customers and let them know that you are there for them if they have questions and that you really exist. Companies need representatives of a business so they are existent. It is hard for a business to gain exposure when they don't have someone to actually talk to.

If your business targets a local community then it is important to get out there and talk to the community. Remember you are looking for the audience who is going to benefit from your product. These are the people you want to talk to.

If you have a business on the web then you will need to get one on one with the customers by providing access to a direct chat option. This gives customers a good feeling but they know that someone really exists. When you offer a direct chat they have the ability to contact a live person rather than talk to a machine. Customers despise machines, automated phone systems, and more. They will try to avoid them and it can give them a bad taste in their mouth about the business. Try to be as responsive as possible with the customers.

Local Business Events

Other local business events are extremely important. Not only do you want to target your local or national audience but you also want to attend other business events. You may find a company struggling that may need your assistance. You might find a company that you can work with together on a project in trade for advertising or even help you build your credibility.

Local business events help you network in the big industry that you may be working in. It is important to talk to companies and let them know you are out there. Maybe you will recommend one company while they recommend you. Always talk to other businesses, let them know about who you are and what you are all about, what their benefit is by knowing you, and how you can help each other. Give them something to remember you by and make an impact.

When you attend events and network with other companies and people then you provide another form of advertising. Networking works very well because when someone does come across a situation where they could use your product or service they will remember you. Creating contacts is a very big part of branding. It also helps instill your company name in the minds of people around the industry.

Chapter 9 – Media Consideration

Media is extremely important when branding a business. There are many different outlets and they can be used in many different ways to your advantage and even for damage control. Proper branding means staying tight with the media as your friend. Some say to keep your friends close and your enemies closer and this is true with the media. They can make you very popular or ruin you but nothing really in between. You need the media on your side at all times.

Local Media

There are many different local media outlets that you might consider using when you are looking to brand your company or a product. You can use local newspapers to announce sales, events, and other things. The television stations are useful when running advertisements or events on the news.

One thing to keep in mind is that public television stations are free and they cannot charge you money to run something on them. If you are a non-profit organization looking to brand your organization the best way to do it is through public television stations. You can announce events like blood drives and other things on public television. This is great exposure and it is free.

Other methods of local media may be local websites for town members. Some towns have a site for the community where people can post things like classified ads and other things. They are free sites and sometimes used more than the newspapers because of this.

Article Writing for Press

Another way you can use the media to your advantage is to write your own articles and distribute them to the press. This is very beneficial. If the press comes across times they need to fill additional space in their paper they may use them.

Sending articles to the press is free. The will not charge you to use them. If you write beneficial articles to magazines in the industry you work in then you may even get paid for the article.

Article writing is a very beneficial way to advertise your business and helps with the branding process.

Sponsors

Looking for sponsors is very important. It is very similar to getting an endorsement. You may make a deal with companies to sponsor you that might include putting up an advertisement at a local event or charity you are holding. Sponsors need to see a benefit in it for them and they are usually willing. When you find local sponsors it helps build credibility with your business. You should always look for local or national sponsors.

Sponsors can be used on your website and at your local business. The most common way to obtain a sponsor is by offering them advertising for their business.

Written Testimonials

Written testimonials are very important in the branding process because they work in two ways. They help build credibility and trust with the targeted audience.

When you sell products or services to customers it is

important to gather as many written testimonials that you can from customers. A customer can write up the type of product or service they purchased from your company and their experience working with you. The more written testimonials you have the better.

Written testimonials are beneficial because they create hype. They increase the excitement about your business and make people want to try your product. Testimonials tell the public that you followed through on delivering the promise made.

Without written testimonials it is hard to prove that you deliver. It is hard to build a brand without people to back you like endorsements through public figures and people in the community.

Special Offers

Building a brand also requires you to provide offers and special discounts to the customers. Customers are always looking for a great deal and when they know they can get it from you they will shop from you.

You might offer discount codes to customers for specific items or even a buy one get one free deal. These are excellent ways to promote a business. If you have an online company then you may offer free shipping or other types of discounts to people during a specified period of time.

Special offers work very well with customers. Free items usually work the best because customers find that nothing is ever free. Although it is not cost effective to give away free items you may include something free with a purchase of a bigger item.

Referrals

Another media consideration when you are building up your brand is that you need to work on referrals. Referrals work very well in building up your brand. This is word of mouth through customers who swear by you. These can be difficult to build up but when you get referrals it helps with credibility.

You can help with gaining referrals to your business by offering specials or discounts to customers that refer you to other customers. This may be a $5 discount on their next purchase or something else. When the customer sees there is a benefit in it for them they will often times refer the company to gain the benefit. This helps increase a customer base, revenues, and build up your brand.

Inserts

Inserts are very beneficial to brand building and a perfect use of the media. Some newspapers or brochures may have a cost associated with adding an insert in a newspaper while others may allow you to provide an insert for free.

Inserts in newspapers and magazines allow for more exposure of the company. Even if a customer doesn't thoroughly read an insert they will remember the name of the company and your logo. It creates a stamp in their mind about you and the products and services offered. This way if they come across a situation where they need a product or your service they will think of the business. Inserts work well and are very beneficial for getting into the mind of customers.

Chapter 10 – The Competitive Edge

Creating a competitive edge is another important aspect of branding. Today, the online world has many methods of branding. The most popular method of branding and gaining the competitive edge is through the use of Blogs. Blogs allow a site to increase traffic, improve rank through search engine results, and even helps with credibility building also.

About Blogs

Blogs are websites that use the new Web 2.0 technology, which allows visitors to a site to post their own comments, articles, and more. Giving a user the access to post things to your site allows them to feel a sense of ownership to the business. They work in many ways, which may include forums, discussion boards, or even look like a daily diary in a sense. They keep the visitors up to date on current events and allow for discussion to take place.

Reasons to Use Blogs

There are many reasons to use blogs for a business. A business may want to provide a discussion board that allows other customers to discuss troubleshooting tips and tricks. A company may post useful information about how to get the most longevity out of products, how to repair or fix things, and even how to prevent problems from occurring.

Using a Blog to Your Benefit

If you do decide to add a blog to your company site then there are many things to consider so you get the most out of it. Some companies allow people to post their own content while others cannot. Consider things like keywords and phrases, links, useful information, and even contact information.

The primary purpose of blog writing for branding is to gain more exposure to a business and get the word out to people that the company exists. Blogs are an excellent way to create hype and exposure because the web has millions of businesses and customers.

When using a blog it is important to make sure that you use important keywords that are relevant to the products and services offered by your business. These keywords and phrases should be the words that will be typed into the search engines when a user is looking for what you offer. The keywords should be used naturally throughout the content of the blog. They will work by allowing your blog to be pulled up in the search engine results when users type in the specific keywords and phrases you used in the blog.

Adding links to blogs is a very important thing for two reasons. They provide an easy method to get back to your site and provide an inbound link. Users always appreciate an easy way to get to your company. If you are talking about products and services offered in a blog without links to where the customers can find them then it will do no good. Customers will only search for a business for a very short period if they search at all. You have a better chance of a customer when a link is right there in the blog so they can easily click and find out more about the company.

URLs are also beneficial for a business because they provide inbound links. One of the ways that search engines work is that one of the ways they rank a business is through popularity. Popularity can be built up by links integrated within blogs. The more inbound links you provide inside of a blog the more popularity a search engine thinks you have. Never forget to place inbound links inside of blogs and content you place on your blog.

A blog needs to provide beneficial information for the visitors and readers. When there is something useful to the reader they will come back for more. Blogs give you the opportunity to give the free advice and useful information that will benefit the users and cause you to gain credibility for being knowledgeable about the products and services offered.

Chapter 12 – Reinforcement of Your Brand

The most important thing about branding is that you need to constantly reinforce the promises you make to the targeted audience. A branding program can be reinforced by being consistent.

Consistency is the most important factor when you reinforce. It shows that you are serious about your brand and your product. It is important to be consistent to show credibility with the customers and the public eye. When a company is not consistent it looks bad for a company as if they are disorganized or have problems.

Reinforcing your brand needs to be done on a regular basis. You should practice constant branding techniques that work for your company. Schedule them weekly or monthly if you have to. For example, try to send out at least two press releases a month to numerous media contacts. Let them know how you are doing and what is going on with the company. Make announcements about ways you better the community and people who use your products.

Reinforcement works for a business with the media also. When you are continuously in contact with the media it will benefit you when something bad happens. Having the media on your side is very important. They will help you with damage control when a customer makes an accusation or if you need assistance with a bad situation.

Reinforcing your brand means that you back what you say you are going to do. You need to prove to the customers that what you say you will do is true and continuously reinforcing this will brand the idea into their minds.

Chapter 13 – Conclusion

Branding is something that every business needs to practice on a daily basis or whenever the opportunity arises. You must work hard to ensure that you make an impact on the way customers think about the products or services offered to the communities.

When you practice branding you need to ensure you are targeting the right audience demographics. Logos are important but they are not your selling point. They just make a statement. Use a tagline along with a logo or with an advertisement only when you think it will grab the attention of customers in a positive way.

Branding requires you to use media outlets to your benefit. You must be proactive in your methods of branding. You can hire someone to do the branding for you. A business has complete control over their brand and their image. The goal of branding is to get into the minds of customers in a positive way and help them realize your business offers a beneficial product to them. You have something that they need.

Branding requires you to separate yourself from the competition proving why the business is the best option to purchase from. There needs to be a clear picture what makes you different, unique, and why a customer should choose you over the competition.

The thing to remember about branding is that it helps produce an image about a business. Consistency is very important. You cannot perform branding by creating a logo on a website and walking away. Branding requires proactive approaches of exposure through article writing, press release distribution, public appearances, products with logos, and much more. Trust and credibility must be built through the branding process. By using these techniques you can be off to an amazing start of building a trustworthy brand that customers can rely on.

Also, always follow through with promises you make to customers through a mission or any statements.

www.ingramcontent.com/pod-product-compliance
Lightning Source LLC
Chambersburg PA
CBHW081806170526
45167CB00008B/3348